D1639661

BUCKINGHAM
A Pictorial History

Church Street, Buckingham

BUCKINGHAM
A Pictorial History

Julian Hunt

Phillimore

1994

Published by
PHILLIMORE & CO. LTD.,
Shopwyke Manor Barn, Chichester, West Sussex
in association with
Buckinghamshire County Library

ISBN 0 85033 941 3

Printed and bound in Great Britain by
BIDDLES LTD.
Guildford, Surrey

List of Illustrations

Frontispiece: Church Street, Buckingham

Acknowledgements

Many of the photographs used in this book are from the large collection assembled over the years by the County Reference Library in Aylesbury. These were supplemented in 1992 with the purchase, by the County Library, of the Buckinghamshire prints accumulated by the former postcard distributors, Francis Frith & Co. Thanks are due to Birmingham Reference Library, where the glass negatives of these prints are preserved, for permission to reproduce those which are still in copyright.

Thanks are also due to the Buckinghamshire Record Office for permission to reproduce the documents numbered 30 and 94-5, to the County Museum, the source of photographs 40 and 67, and to the Bucks Archaeological Society for the copy of the print numbered 120. The Royal Commission on Historic Monuments, whose photographic collection has recently been moved to new premises in Swindon, supplied photographs 13-14, 18, 23, 37, 47-8, 51, 57, 65, 70, 72, 82 and 125. Mr. J. H. Venn of Great Missenden supplied prints from the negatives of the late Stanley Freese. These are numbered 10, 59, 63, 88 and 107 whilst number 112 is from Mr. Venn's own collection. Messrs Chapman, photographers, Buckingham, are the source of photograph number 111. The Guildhall Library, London, supplied the copy of the insurance policy reproduced as number 53, and the University of Buckingham has given permission to reproduce photograph number 71. Mr. Sam Grigg loaned photographs 113-14, Mr. Alan Petford took the photographs numbered 33-4, 75, 91 and 143-4 and Mr. Ian Toplis provided illustration number 140.

Particular thanks are due to the staffs of the County Reference Library and the County Record Office, where the bulk of the research for this book was carried out.

Introduction

The Origin of Buckingham

'The place of Bucca's people hemmed in by water' is the literal meaning of the place-name 'Buckingham'. We will never know who Bucca was or how long his followers had lived there, but we do know that, in 914, their humble settlement became of great military importance. In that year, Edward the Elder fortified the spur of land around which the Ouse curves as a stronghold in the campaign against the Danes. The success of his strategy meant that, within thirty years, the two 'burghs' or fortifications he built were redundant, but their locations are evidenced by the area name of Bourtonhold and the hamlet name of Bourton.

The date of the fortification of Buckingham is given in the Anglo-Saxon Chronicle. How such a fortress was manned and financed is described in a document called the Burghal Hidage which must have been compiled or revised around 914. Here Buckingham is ranked with other fortified towns in Southern England which are vital to the campaign against the Danes. The Burghal Hidage reckoned that Oxford would need 1,500 hides for its defence, Wallingford 2,400 hides and Buckingham 1,600 hides, each hide providing one man. The hide was a unit of taxation of arable land, perhaps 120 acres or as much as one family could maintain. The compiler stated that 160 men could defend a furlong (220 yards) of a town's wall. Buckingham's allocation of 1,600 hides suggests perimeter defences of the two burghs extending to 10 furlongs in total or over half a mile each.

The foundation of Buckinghamshire must coincide with the fortification of Buckingham and the compilation of the Burghal Hidage. The county boundary includes those parishes whose taxation of 1,600 hides was allocated to Buckingham in 914, plus the villages immediately to the north of Buckingham, whose taxes were paid to the Danes before 914, and also the settlements in the Chilterns whose hidage was originally set aside for a fortification on the Thames, named in the Burghal Hidage as Sceaftesige.

Buckingham in Domesday Book

By the time of the Norman Conquest, Buckingham was a royal borough with 53 burgesses, a mint, a well-endowed church and two valuable mills. The fact that it is only rated at one hide in Domesday Book suggests that newcomers had been offered the most advantageous terms to invest in the new borough. This view is supported by an analysis of 27 of the burgesses who are tenants not of the king but of the lords of several manors surrounding Buckingham.

Before the conquest, four burgesses had been tenants of Alric, son of Goding, a thegn of King Edward. Alric was lord of Beachampton, Bourton, Hillesden, Lenborough and Maids Moreton. At the conquest all these manors passed to Hugh de Bolbec as tenant of Walter Giffard and with them went the rents of the four burgesses in Buckingham. Five more burgesses paid their rent to Azor, son of Toti, often described as a man of Edward's Queen, Edith. He was the lord of Quainton, Radclive, Shalston Thornton and Water Stratford. In 1086 these manors had passed to new Norman landlords, Roger d'Oilly and Roger de Ivry, and with them went the rents of the same burgesses in Buckingham.

In fact all the rents of Buckingham burgesses can be linked to surrounding manors as if their lords were obliged to place a trusted man in the town. This may have been a military arrangement, like the Burghal Hidage, but the intention was more likely to ensure the commercial development of the new borough. The fact that nearby Lamport (meaning a long market) became a mere hamlet of Stowe suggests that the centre of trade of the area was moved into the new borough of Buckingham to guarantee its survival.

Even royal boroughs need farmers to supply their markets and feed their inhabitants and Domesday Book gives a good description of Buckingham's agricultural land. King William's manorial farm there had two ploughs working (needing 16 oxen) and a mill to grind his tenants' corn. Besides 26 burgesses, his tenants included an unspecified number of villeins (or tenant farmers) who had between them three-and-a-half ploughs (needing 28 oxen), 11 bordars (or smallholders) and two serfs (or labourers). The assessors concluded that there was land for two-and-a-half more ploughs for there was pasture for all the livestock of the town and enough meadow to feed eight plough teams (64 oxen).

Domesday Book gives prominence to the property originally given as an endowment for the important church at Buckingham. This land was later to be called the Prebend End, after the Prebendary of Sutton *cum* Buckingham, an ecclesiastic at Lincoln Cathedral to whom the income was later paid. In 1066 it belonged to Wulfwig, Bishop of Dorchester. By 1086 it had passed to Remigius, Bishop of Lincoln, who had made Lincoln the centre of his diocese in 1072. There was suffcient land in the Bishop's part of Buckingham for four ploughs. His tenants comprised three villeins, three bordars and 10 cottars (or cottagers) who had four ploughs between them and he had a mill where they would be required to grind their corn. There was only enough meadow to support two plough teams and adequate woodland for making fences. The Bishop is also listed as owning the hamlet of Gawcott, assessed at one hide. Here two bordars and one serf had a further one-and-a-half ploughs, but there was only enough meadow to feed half a plough team. It is worth noting that the church land was short of meadow for three ploughs, whilst the assessors found excess meadowland in Buckingham with Bourton amounting to two-and-a-half teams.

The parish of Buckingham includes the hamlets of Bourton and Lenborough, both of which are mentioned in Domesday. Bourton (probably the second fortification referred to in the Anglo-Saxon Chronicle) belonged in 1066 to Alric, a thegn of King Edward. In 1086 the powerful Walter Giffard held Bourton which was rated at one hide. His tenant Hugh de Bolbec had a manorial farm employing one plough. Hugh's sub-tenants comprised two villeins and two bordars who had a second plough and there was enough meadow to feed the two plough teams.

Alric had also held part of Lenborough, rated at three hides, and was succeeded here, as in Bourton, by Walter Giffard's follower, Hugh de Bolbec. Hugh had a manorial farm employing one plough. Two bordars had another plough and there was sufficient meadow land for the two teams. Alric and Hugh de Bolbec after him were the sponsors of four burgesses in Buckingham.

The remaining part of Lenborough, assessed at seven hides, had belonged to Wilaf, a man of Earl Leofwine (King Harold's brother). In 1086 it was held by Ernulf de Hesding as tenant to the bishop of Bayeux. Their manorial farm had two ploughs at work and one villein, six bordars and three serfs had another plough, but there was enough land and meadow to support two more. There is mention of woodland worth four shillings a year. Wilaf and Ernulf de Hesding his successor were responsible for one burgess in the town.

Taking the Domesday assessments of the component parts together, we find the parish of Buckingham having 101 taxable individuals, which suggests a population in excess of five hundred. The hidage was 13, giving an acreage of arable land of 1,560, on which there were 17½ ploughs at work. There were two water mills to grind the corn. There was adequate meadowland but little woodland.

The Manor of Buckingham

The Normans probably took over the fortifications at Buckingham and may well have built their own castle there. Soon after Domesday, King William II gave Buckingham to Walter Giffard, the biggest landowner in the county whose principal estate was at Long Crendon. Walter Giffard was made Earl of Buckingham but neither he nor any other overlord was ever resident at Buckingham. The castle was never occupied and may soon have fallen into disrepair again. The male line of Giffards ceased with the next generation and Buckingham passed down the female line.

Buckingham is next glimpsed in 1279 when the Hundred Rolls, under the heading 'Buckingham Castle', record that William de Breuse 'holds this tenement by a knight's fee of William de Breuse his father and the same William of the Earl of Gloucester and the same Earl holds in chief of the King and the Honour of Giffard'. In a reference to what must be the Castle Mill, the document continues: 'William de Breuse holds three carucates of land in demesne and has free fishing ... from the mill as far as the end of the pond. John de Breuse holds one watermill of the said William. Item Robert de Morten holds of the said William 30 acres of land'.

By the 15th century, the manor of Buckingham had passed to Humphrey Stafford, the first to enjoy the title of Duke of Buckingham. After the third Duke, Edward Stafford, was executed for treason in 1521, Buckingham reverted to the Crown. It was purchased in 1552 by Robert Brocas of Horton, near Edlesborough, and it was his son Bernard Brocas who sold off the Castle Farm and Castle Mill and leased the manorial rights to the Corporation of Buckingham in 1573.

Buckingham Charter, 1554

In 1554, the newly-crowned Mary Tudor granted a charter of incorporation to Buckingham, one of the first towns to proclaim her Queen on the death of Edward VI. The town had long enjoyed borough status but now its rights were confirmed by a royal charter. The Corporation was to receive the tolls of a Tuesday market and two annual fairs and was to hold borough courts to try commercial actions up to the value of five pounds. It was to be run by a bailiff and 12 elected burgesses who in turn were to elect two representatives to sit in Parliament for the borough. The limits of the borough were stated as from Dudley bridge on the west to Thornborough bridge on the east and from Chackmore brook on the north to Padbury Mill bridge on the south; that is, the entire parish of Buckingham.

It was this raising of the status of Buckingham which may have induced the Corporation to lease the manorial rights from the lord of the manor, Bernard Brocas, in 1573. Six members of the Corporation were party to the deed; Raphael Moore, yeoman, John Lambert the younger, butcher, Henry Miller, yeoman, John Fowks, mercer, Robert Shyne, baker and George Apowell, bellfounder. The term of the lease was 2,000 years and the rent was

40s. per year. Brocas sold the right to collect this 40s. to two of his Bedfordshire neighbours, Thomas and Richard Neale, who in 1604 sold it to Sir Thomas Temple. Thus began the influence over town affairs by the Temple-Grenville family of Stowe which was to last for over 250 years. In this book, successive heads of this family are referred to by their contemporary titles, such as Lord Cobham, Earl Temple, the Marquis of Buckingham and the Duke of Buckingham.

The Castle Farm

Before letting the manor as a whole, Bernard Brocas gave many of his tenants 2,000-year leases on their houses. The deeds to many houses on the Market Hill and in Bourton Hold start with a lease from Brocas in 1574. These houses can be equated with the burgess tenements of the king at Domesday. Houses that are ancient freeholds are more likely to have been tenements belonging at Domesday to the lords of the manor of the surrounding parishes. At the same time as the manorial rights were sold, Bernard Brocas sold the Castle Farm to the tenant, Francis Dayrell of Lamport, near Stowe. The farm included land dispersed in three fields to the north of Buckingham which were sown and harvested in common by all the farmers of the town. In the same conveyance of 1576, Brocas sold to Dayrell the two water mills called the Castle Mills and four acres of meadow or pasture upstream from the mills where the farmhouse probably stood. The recently restored Corner House on West Street may well be on the site of the Castle Farm.

The Castle Farm land passed from the Dayrells to the family of Lord Sackville of Drayton in Northamptonshire. The strips of land scattered in the open fields were gradually enclosed by purchase and exchange and, after the enclosure of nearby Chackmore in 1773, the Grenvilles were able to lay out the broad avenue from the Brackley Road to the Corinthian Arch at Stowe. The Marquis of Buckingham bought up the Sackville property in about 1803 and a new farm, Castle Fields, was built to the east of the avenue.

The Prebend End of Buckingham

At Domesday, the church of Buckingham was endowed with land to the south of the town including the hamlet of Gawcott. The bishop of Lincoln gave the income from this land to a prebendary at Lincoln who also received the income of church property at Kings Sutton in Northamptonshire. The centre of the church land in Buckingham was the Prebendal House and mill which stood to the south east of the old churchyard. The Prebendal House was probably the finest in the town and the tenant would be obliged to house the prebendary and his retinue should he visit the manor to hold a court or preach in the parish church. Queen Elizabeth was entertained to lunch there when journeying from Towcester to Bicester in 1568.

After the Reformation no more prebendaries were appointed and their property was taken over by the Crown. In 1613, the Prebend End of Buckingham and Gawcott, including the Prebendal House and 240 acres of land dispersed in the common fields, was sold to Sir Thomas Denton of Hillesden. The mill, which still stands, was sold separately. Hillesden House was sacked by the Parliamentary army during the Civil War and it may well be that the Prebendal House was destroyed at the same time. Certainly it had been pulled down by 1654 when the Dentons sold the land 'whereon the Prebend or Parsonage House there did lately stand'.

The house now called Manor House which overlooks the old churchyard was a large farmhouse which by 1751 was leased from the Dentons by the Grenvilles of Stowe. For many years the Grenvilles sublet the house as a private girls' school, but when the Duke of Buckingham purchased the manor of the Prebend End and Gawcott in 1824 he began to hold his manorial courts there and it acquired the name Manor House. Right up to modern times, tenants in the Prebend End of Buckingham held their farms and houses by copyhold; that is they kept a copy of the court roll for the year in which they inherited or bought their property. This type of tenure lasted until 1926 when government legislation forced remaining copyhold landlords to sell the freeholds to the tenants.

The Civil War
Unlike Aylesbury and Newport Pagnell, which were garrisoned by the Parliamentarians during the Civil War, Buckingham was not a stronghold for either side. Sir Richard Minshull of Bourton, unpopular as a Catholic and for depopulating Bourton by enclosure in the 1630s, had his house destroyed by local Parliamentarians even before the war began. Sir Edmund Verney of Claydon felt obliged to support the king but died carrying the royal standard at Edge Hill in 1642. His son, Sir Ralph Verney, fled to France but faced heavy fines after the war for his 'delinquency'. Sir Alexander Denton of Hillesden allowed his house to be fortified as a Royalist outpost with the result that it was attacked and destroyed by the Parliamentarians in 1643. His neighbour, Sir Richard Ingoldsby of Lenborough, sided with Parliament. Sir Richard Temple was also active on the Parliamentary side, yet he continued to improve his estates, completing the enclosure of Stowe by 1649. With the Parliamentarians holding London and the King's court established at Oxford, Buckingham was vulnerable to raids by both sides in search of money and provisions. Oliver Cromwell stayed at Buckingham after the siege of Hillesden in March 1643/4, whilst King Charles briefly occupied the town, staying at the Lamberts' old home, Castle House, in June 1644.

The Fire of Buckingham
Until the 18th century, Buckingham's houses were built mostly of timber with lath and plaster or brick panels. Some buildings were tiled but most, especially the outhouses, were thatched. Some of the tradesmen had fire insurance policies with firms like the Sun Fire Office, but most houses were not insured. In March 1724/5, a fire broke out behind the *Unicorn Inn* near the Market Square. It spread along both sides of Castle Street and consumed most of the houses on the north side of Well Street. In all, 138 houses were destroyed, making over 500 people homeless. The tradesmen whose property had been spared promptly took out fire insurance, as did many inhabitants of neighbouring towns. Lord Cobham erected a block of brick-built houses across the end of the Cow Fair to house those who could not rebuild their own homes. Buckingham was slow to rebuild after the fire and the opportunity to lay out new streets was not taken.

The Summer Assizes
In 1748, a concerted attempt was made to win back the status of county town which had been lost to Aylesbury. A private Act of Parliament was passed fixing Buckingham as the place for holding the summer assizes and Lord Cobham paid for the building of a new gaol on the Market Hill. Its thick stone walls surmounted by battlements were designed to reassure the sceptical that Buckingham had the resources to host this important county function. It was unfortunate that a new County Hall in Aylesbury, paid for by a rate imposed on the whole county, had only recently been completed, with far superior facilities

both for the judges and the prisoners. The summer assizes were nonetheless held in Buckingham and the gaol was extended in 1839 with accommodation for the Superintendent of Buckingham police force which had been set up three years earlier. In 1849, however, Aylesbury promoted its own Act of Parliament, repealing the 1748 Act and returning the assizes to Aylesbury once and for all.

The Enclosure of the Prebend End and Gawcott, 1803

Unlike the farmland attached to the Borough of Buckingham, the arable land in the Prebend End and Gawcott was organised on the open field system until the beginning of the 19th century. There were three fields in the Prebend End; to the north east was the Great Port Field, to the east was the Little Port Field and to the south east was Buckingham Field. In Gawcott, the Wood Field was to the north west of the village, the Middle Field to the north east and the Little Field to the south.

The private Act of Parliament of 1801, appointing commissioners to reallocate the open field land of the Prebend End and Gawcott, also provided for the enclosure of the parish of Maids Moreton. The common factor was the Marquis of Buckingham, who was part lord of the manor of Maids Moreton, and owned the right to collect the tithes of the Prebend End and Gawcott where he was also a copyhold tenant of several houses and farms. The commissioners awarded him 195 acres out of 1,328 acres surveyed. Other beneficiaries were John Bartlett and Alexander Norton, who both owned tanneries in the Prebend End, and William Eagles, a copyhold tenant of one of the largest farms in Gawcott. Their land was no longer in strips scattered around the three fields of the parish but was laid out in neat blocks, in the case of William Eagles, directly behind his farm-house. In Maids Moreton, All Souls College, Oxford, which was part lord of the manor, also benefited and built College Farm on land which had previously been the common arable land of the parish.

Buckingham as a coaching centre

Ogilby's maps of the principal coaching roads, first published in 1675, shows Buckingham as a crossroads. The road from London to Banbury and the Midlands reaches Buckingham from Aylesbury via Quarrendon, East Claydon and Padbury and continues to Banbury via Tingewick. The Oxford to Cambridge Road approaches Buckingham from the south west, passing below Tingewick and entering the town via the Prebend End. These maps were sold to the upper classes and to merchants and carriers and were available at the coaching inns.

Later maps show that Buckingham became even more of a crossroads in the turnpike era. The Buckingham to Wendover Turnpike Act of 1720 named commissioners drawn largely from the local gentry who were to set up tollgates along the route and apply the income to road repairs. Initially the turnpike road took the old coaching route from Aylesbury to Buckingham via East Claydon, crossing the Ouzel on the Ox Lane bridge at Padbury. A second Act of Parliament in 1742 provided for a new Padbury bridge further downstream and the turnpike from Aylesbury now passed through Whitchurch and Winslow. Other improvements followed, such as the diversion avoiding the descent and climb in and out of Padbury village built after 1796, the rebuilding of Padbury bridge in 1827 and the diversion of the road to the new bridge over the Ouse at Buckingham in 1805. These diversions are often marked by the building of public houses, such as the *New Inn*, Padbury, and the *New Inn*, London Road, Buckingham. Nearly all the main roads into Buckingham were turnpiked; the Buckingham to Warmington Road via Tingewick in 1744, the Buckingham to Brackley Road in 1791, the Buckingham to Newport Pagnell Road in 1815 and the Towcester Road in 1824. Milestones erected by the turnpike trustees remain on all these roads but their tollhouses were all demolished after the last turnpike acts expired in the late Victorian period.

Coaching inns required ample accommodation both for travellers and their horses. The inns usually had elegant façades facing the street with tall archways leading to the coach and stable yard. An ostler would be on hand to look after the horses, and establishments which were advertised as 'posting houses' would hire out horses to pull coaches to similar inns in the next large town. Buckingham had at least four such inns, all of them rebuilt during the 18th century when the coaching trade was reaching its peak. These were the *White Hart* in the Market Square, the *Swan and Castle* in Castle Street, the *Cobham Arms* in West Street and the *George* in High Street. The opening of the London to Birmingham Railway in 1838 marked the end of the coaching era. Coaches plied between Buckingham and Wolverton until the Buckingham branch line opened in 1850. The *Cobham Arms*, owned by and named after Richard Temple, created Lord Cobham in 1714, closed in 1856. The *George Inn* became a private house and is now called the White House, accommodating local authority offices. The *White Hart* had its central coach entrance converted into a lobby, but the *Swan and Castle* retains its broad coach entrance.

The Grand Junction Canal

The Grand Junction Canal, opened in 1799, was one of the nation's most profitable canals. It linked London and Birmingham and boasted double 14ft.-wide locks to speed the barges on their way, and pumping engines so that the water lost as each lock was emptied could be returned to the higher level. The branches provided to Aylesbury and Buckingham were built with seven-foot locks, requiring the transhipment of goods from barges to narrow boats. The Buckingham branch was opened in 1801 amid great celebration, but the effect on the town's economy was not dramatic. The wharf was some way to the east of the town, where ruined canal cottages remain in 1994, but it was soon extended into the North East End where a new wharf with wharfinger's house was built. For some years it provided cheaper coal and enabled the turnpike trustees to import better quality stone for road surfacing. Welsh slate began to replace local tiles as the normal roofing material and the larger slates enabled builders to construct rooves of shallower pitch.

The Branch Railway Line

Whilst Aylesbury was reached by a branch line from the London to Birmingham Railway in 1839, Buckingham had to wait until 1850 for a station on a similar branch from Bletchley to Banbury. Economies dictated that it should be a single track line and, as with the canal, the commercial impact on Buckingham was limited. It could be argued that the railway led to the further decline of Buckingham's market as the town was no longer the only option for farmers selling their produce in north-west Buckinghamshire. The railway prompted at least one new enterprise—the Castle Iron Works—an agricultural machinery works set up in 1857 as a limited liability company by a group of local tradesmen. It was run by a gifted engineer called Thomas Rickett who proved better at designing primitive steam cars than building a local market for the firm's goods. The factory, built near the railway station, was sold in 1865 and became a steam-powered corn mill before being converted into a condensed milk factory.

Trade and Industry

With no raw materials to exploit, Buckingham lived by trade passing through its market. Only freemen of the borough were able to trade in the market—outsiders could only trade here after paying a considerable sum to one of four guilds. In 1663 it was £15 to join the mercers' company which included grocers, haberdashers, linen and woollen drapers, clothiers, silkmen and goldsmiths. It cost £6 to join the tailors, that is dyers, fullers, weavers, smiths, glasiers, pewterers, brasiers, fletchers, furbishers and painters. The cordwainers charged £9 to shoemakers, tanners, fellmongers, glovers, parchment makers, saddlers, girdle makers, collar makers, point makers and bottle makers for admission, whilst the butchers, including bakers, cooks and millers, charged £6. Each guild appointed wardens to ensure that only their members set up stalls in the market and sold goods of the correct measure and quality.

In 1684, market day was changed to Saturday. Parts of the market place were set aside for different trades. A wool hall stood on the north side of the Market Square near to the *Fleece Inn*. This was replaced by a butchers' shambles in 1814. The shops from the *Fleece Inn* to West Street were called Butchers' Row. In the centre of the market place was the Bull Ring, still occupied by a group of shops near the old gaol. The part of the market area north-east of the gaol was called the Cow Fair.

Buckingham was not a noted corn market, but the Ouse powered three large corn mills, the Castle Mill, the Town Mill and Bourton Mill, all three of which added steam engines and continued to operate into the present century. The Castle Mill was rebuilt as late as 1897 by Alfred Charles Rogers who also ran the Town Mill and the Station Mill, a failed agricultural machinery works which he converted into a steam-powered corn mill. These mills may also have played their part in a small domestic woollen industry, for the bridge by the Castle Mill is called the Fullingmere bridge in 1797. Water power is used in such mills to raise fulling hammers which compact the fibres in newly woven cloth. The Town Mill is marked as a fulling mill on Jeffery's map of 1770 and the datestone on the east wall, WK 1782, relates to William King, variously described as a miller and dyer.

The larger farmers had maltings such as those near Castle House and on the Lenborough Road and the Stuchbery family had an old established brewery in the North East End of the town. The Duke of Buckingham also owned a brewery on West Street which was let in the 1870s to John Terry, son of Edward Terry, Aylesbury's wealthiest brewer. Most of the pubs supplied by Terry belonged to the Duke, so the brewery was unable to compete with larger concerns like the Aylesbury Brewery Company, which had a much larger number of tied pubs in the area.

Towns with large cattle markets are bound to have tanneries and other trades associated with leather. Some of Buckingham's tanneries were once situated to the south east of the Market Square where the river provided plenty of water to wash the skins. By the 18th century the trade had become concentrated in the Prebend End where there was more space for expansion and direct access to the river. The principal tanners here throughout the 18th century were the Nortons, whose house on Hunter Street is now occupied by the University of Buckingham and after whom the nearby cottages called Norton's Row are named. Alexander Norton died in 1816 and the tanyard was continued by his son-in-law, Isaac Shortland Bartlett, until his own death in 1833. A measure of Buckingham's decline is that these once productive premises were for many years after used as a hunting box.

The rival tan yards to the south of this were bought up in the mid-18th century by the Bartlett family who came from Brackley, where they had been skinners and fellmongers for several generations. Robert Bartlett (1723-79) was bailiff of Buckingham in 1777 and laid the foundation stone of the new church on Castle Hill. At his death he divided his tanyards between his sons Edward (1756-95), whose family continued to run a tannery and woolstapling business behind the present Yeomanry House, and John Bartlett (1763-1826), who built Prebend House and operated the tannery behind the present Istra Cottages. A huge wooden building, which was attached to these cottages and must have been used for hanging skins, was only demolished in 1974.

The Bartletts became partners in Philip Box's Buckingham Bank and set up their own bank in 1811 when Box died. They sold their tanyard in 1851 to Humphrey Humphreys, a tanner from Dover, whose son ran it for a while. The last tenant, and thus the last tanner in business in Buckingham, was William Sowerby, who was in occupation as late as 1868.

After tanning, leather is dressed and coloured by the currier. The leading currying concern in the town was run by William Walker of Bristle Hill whose yard was probably on School Lane. He employed 20 men there in 1851. William Walker was a keen supporter of the Congregational chapel in Church Street.

The last woolstapling concern in Buckingham was run by Frederick Edward Bartlett (1818-1902), who employed up to 20 men in the work. The trade was very long established in Buckingham; the *Woolpack Inn* in Well Street is an ancient inn and there had been a wool hall in the Market Square prior to 1814 when a new butcher's market was built on part of the site. The job of sorting wool was continued in Bartlett's yard until the Yorkshire woollen spinners practice of buying fleeces direct from the farmer killed the trade. Frederick Bartlett finally sold the wool yard to the Royal Bucks Hussars in 1886. His home thus became known as Yeomanry House, and is now occupied by the University of Buckingham.

The making of shoes is a domestic industry common to most towns and villages but the concentration of the trade in Northampton led many to apply the same economies of scale to production in local towns like Olney and Buckingham. Henry Holland built a four-storey shoe factory behind the Market Square in about 1850. It is built of a fine yellow brick that was used locally only after the railways made transport cheap enough. There were already 76 men employed by 1851. The business was carried on into this century by Henry Holland's son Rechab. The shoe factory is described in Flora Thompson's *Lark Rise to Candleford*. It has recently been converted into flats.

The domestic lace industry was conducted vigorously in this area, with most wives of agricultural labourers supplementing or even exceeding their husband's income. The lace buyers went from cottage to cottage supplying the raw materials and patterns and taking the product to distant markets. Newman Williat, Bailiff of Buckingham in 1785, 1790 and 1804, and owner of Trolley Hall, was a wealthy lace buyer.

Buckingham Banks

Tradesmen in market towns often turned to wealthy drapers to borrow money and to finance new enterprises, often by giving a mortgage on their property as security. A class of financiers thus emerged, some of whom began to call themselves bankers. Philip Box, a draper in Market Hill, set up a bank in 1786. George Parrott of Castle Fields Farm, the agent to the Grenvilles of Stowe, became a partner in the bank, as did John Bartlett (1763-1826) and Edward Bartlett (1756-95), two brothers who owned the largest of the tan yards on Hunter Street.

On the death of Philip Box in 1811, his nephew, also called Philip Box, carried on the banking business with George Parrott whilst John Bartlett set up a rival bank in partnership with his former clerk, George Nelson. The split probably came about for good business reasons, but the two banks also represented the two political camps in Buckingham. The Grenvilles of Stowe, supported by Parrott, were determined to maintain control of Buckingham's Corporation whose 12 burgesses elected two M.P.s, whilst Bartlett and Nelson wished to assert the town's independence.

During the 1820s, public confidence in small banks was damaged by widespread failures, and Box and Parrott was forced to close in 1821. In 1824, the Buckingham mail coach, carrying a parcel of money from Bartlett's Bank to Praed & Co. of London, was held up by highwaymen. George Parrott had resumed banking by 1830 and went into partnership with his former rivals as Bartlett, Parrott and Company in 1835. The partnership included Edward Bartlett's son Thomas (1795-1850), John Bartlett's son Edward (1798-1835), as well as the solicitor Thomas Hearn of Castle House. By 1853, Bartlett Parrott & Co. was run by a new generation, including Edward Bartlett's son John Edward (1824-88) and George Parrott's son Edward. It was these men who joined with T. R. Cobb of Banbury, and the Aylesbury Old Bank to form the Bucks & Oxon Union Bank in 1853. The bank's headquarters were in Buckingham, and there were branches in most towns in the two counties. Their bank at Winslow, rebuilt in 1891, still bears the B&OUB datestone. Lloyds Bank took over the Bucks and Oxon Union Bank in 1902.

Churches and Chapels
Buckingham church is prominent in Domesday Book which values the land in Buckingham and Gawcott which was set aside for its maintenance. Shortly after Domesday Book was compiled, the income from these lands in Buckingham was coupled with those of Kings Sutton and Horley in Northamptonshire to support a prebendary, a religious official at the cathedral in Lincoln. Until 1445, when Buckingham was given its own vicar, the church was officially a chapelry under the much smaller church of Kings Sutton. When Henry VIII sold off these lands with other church property, no further prebendaries were appointed, but the lay owner of the Prebend End and Gawcott retained the right to appoint the vicar.

Buckingham church was a large cruciform building with a tower at the junction of the transepts, nave and chancel. The wooden steeple, covered in lead and rising to a height of 163ft., collapsed during a gale in February 1698-99, severely damaging the tower. It was not until 1753, due to the exertions of Brown Willis of Whaddon Hall, Buckingham's first historian, that the tower was rebuilt. Unfortunately, this too collapsed in 1776 and it was resolved to build a completely new church.

The Verneys of Claydon were persuaded to donate a site on top of the Castle Hill for the new church and much of the cost of building was met by the Grenvilles of Stowe. The foundation stone was laid in 1777 by Robert Bartlett, tanner, then Bailiff of Buckingham. The new church, consecrated in 1781, was in the form of a large preaching room, with galleries on three sides, facing a tall three-decker pulpit. There was no chancel. The substantial tower was surmounted by an elegant stone-built steeple which is still Buckingham's chief landmark.

The design of Buckingham's new church did not suit the Victorians who put more emphasis on liturgy than on preaching. The Gawcott-born architect George Gilbert Scott was invited to report on the state of the building in 1860. He condemned the foundations as inadequate and prescribed the huge buttresses which now support the outer walls. A chancel, paid for by the Duke of Buckingham, was added in 1865 and, inside, the galleries were ripped out and the pulpit moved to a less prominent position. The church was thus transformed from a classical preaching house to a high gothic church, but the tower remained unaltered.

George Gilbert Scott (1811-1878) was the son of the Rev. Thomas Scott, the first curate of Gawcott. A chapel was built in Gawcott in 1802 at the expense of a local lace buyer named John West, but the chapel was not consecrated until 1806. Thomas Scott himself designed a replacement for this modest structure which was completed in 1827. Like Buckingham church, it was in the classical style, then going out of fashion. The curate's son went on to be the leading church architect of his day and he or his firm were responsible for much of the church rebuilding which was carried out in this area during the Victorian period.

The puritanical zeal and opposition to the established church, which was one of the causes of the Civil War, did not disappear at the restoration of Charles II. The King made several laws to curtail and then to license non-conformity and religious meetings were often held in the houses or barns of the wealthier members of local Baptist, Presbyterian and Independent congregations. The meeting house at the top of Well Street can trace its history to the formation of a Presbyterian congregation about 1700. If they did build a permanent meeting house, then it would have been destroyed in the fire of Buckingham in 1724-25. Part of the structure dates from 1726, but the front wall was moved nearer to the street in a 19th-century extension, probably re-using the original window openings. From 1844 to 1876, the chapel was used to house Buckingham's British School. The building is now used as a garage.

In 1792, part of the Well Street congregation broke away and in the following year built a new chapel in the Church Street garden of Alice Bull, one of the members. The two Independent congregations together promoted the British School in the Well Street premises in 1844, reunited in 1850. In 1857, the chapel in Church Street was replaced by the present gothic building now used as a lecture hall by the University of Buckingham.

The Society of Friends certainly had members in Buckingham in the 17th century but it was not until 1786 that they built a meeting house in the garden of a house next to the *Trooper Inn* on the north side of the Cow Fair or High Street. The most prominent members were the Coles, millers at Castle Mill and bakers here on the Cow Fair. When this family died out, the meeting house ceased to function, but their burial ground is shown on the 1925 map and a part of the meeting house survives as a garden wall.

The Methodists built a chapel on Well Street in 1792 and added schoolrooms and other extensions during the 19th century. The building survived until a new Methodist church, still in use, was built in 1968. The Baptists were not strong in Buckingham, but built the chapel on the Moreton Road in 1842. Although they took some members from the Independents, their numbers soon dwindled and in 1876 their building was used as a Board School until the school in Well Street was completed in 1879. It was later occupied by the Primitive Methodists, but from 1916 it has belonged to the Salvation Army.

Schools

There is some doubt as to the antiquity of Buckingham's Royal Latin School. It has been claimed to be the oldest school in the county, but there is no evidence that a schoolmaster recorded in 1423 as paying rent to his landlord, John Barton, had anything to do with the Latin School. Another suggested date of foundation is 1540, when Isobel Denton of Hillesden left money for the priest in charge of the chantry chapel on the Market Hill to supplement his income by teaching local children. Chantry chapels were common in medieval towns. Their priests said masses for the souls of townsmen, both living and dead, in the hope of ensuring their eternal salvation. When chantry chapels were suppressed by Henry VIII in the 1540s, the priest at Buckingham was pensioned off, but the school is thought to have continued in the chapel and the names of the masters are given by Brown Willis, beginning with Henry Webster in 1553.

The masters of the Latin School tended to be local curates or incumbents of local churches who were glad to supplement their incomes. A new master's house, also paid for by the Dentons, was built in 1696. This house, along with some late 19th-century classrooms built on its north end, are now in private ownership, but the chapel, which had so long served as the schoolroom, is now maintained by the National Trust. Following the Education Act of 1902, the County Council was enabled to support old endowed grammar schools, and a new school was built on Chandos Road in 1907. This building is now a primary school, the Royal Latin School having moved in 1963 to Brookfield, a large house to the south of Chandos Road which had been built as a hunting box, its location near to the railway station being ideal for a London businessman to indulge an interest in field sports.

Large scale educational provision in Buckingham began with the National School, built in 1819 on the street connecting West Street and Nelson Street. It was promoted by the National Society for the Education of the Poor in the Principles of the Established Church. It is clear from the name that the school would not appeal to non-Conformist parents. The original school was rebuilt in 1856 but was still a single-storey building of stone. An infants school was started in 1863 on the opposite side of the road. The prospect of a non-denominational board school being built after the 1870 Education Act spurred the managers to enlarge the school by putting on an extra storey. The girls occupied the upper floor and the boys remained in the original part. The 1872 datestone remains on the upper storey which is built of brick. The school remained in use until the new Secondary School on the London Road was built in 1935.

In 1844, the non-Conformists in the town established a British School, supported by the British and Foreign Schools Society, at the old meeting house in Well Street. When an elected School Board was started following the 1870 Education Act, there was much argument in the town as to whether further school places were needed. The Board pressed on, taking over the British School premises in 1872 and moving the children to the former Baptist Chapel on Moreton Road in 1876. It was not until 1879 that a purpose-built Board School in Well Street was opened. Control of the Board School passed to the county council in 1905. The county now offered a few of the brighter children scholarships to attend the Royal Latin School. The headmaster at Well Street complained that he lost the opportunity to show what he could do with the most promising pupils. With the opening of the Secondary School in 1935, the school in Well street taught primary-age children only. It finally closed in 1991.

The Secondary School, built on the London Road in 1935, aimed to teach 11 to 14 year-olds a more practical curriculum than that offered at the Royal Latin School. With the raising of the school leaving age and the move nationally to comprehensive education, plans were made in the 1970s to merge the two secondary schools. These plans were set aside after the election of the 1979 Conservative government under Margaret Thatcher.

Margaret Thatcher was also a strong supporter of the independent University of Buckingham, opened in 1976. She is now Chancellor of the University. This institution was many years in the planning and came to Buckingham partly through the enthusiasm of Fred Pooley, then Buckinghamshire's County Architect and Planning Officer, who had also developed the concept of the new city at Milton Keynes. The University can claim partial credit for the revival of the town in the 1980s and has preserved and enhanced many fine buildings in the Prebend End of Buckingham.

The Influence of Stowe

In 1554, Sir Peter Temple, a large landowner in Warwickshire, leased an estate at Stowe which before the Dissolution had belonged to the Oxfordshire Abbey of Oseney. His son, Sir John Temple, purchased the freehold of Stowe in 1591. The Temples' increasing wealth came partly from enclosing their estates and transforming parishes like Stowe into great sheep walks. A survey of the Temple estate in 1633 shows that Stowe and Lamport were still open-field villages, with tenant farmers holding their arable land in strips scattered around the three fields of each hamlet. Dadford, by contrast, had already been enclosed, with the farmers' new closes individually named. Stowe, where 77 adult males signed the Protestation Return in 1641, was enclosed in 1649 and the population dwindled rapidly as more and more land was turned over to pasture.

The Temples' fortune increased through the efficient farming of their English estates, the acquisition of sugar plantations in the West Indies, the accumulation of government sinecures and the arrangement of successful marriages. The marriage of the heiress Hester Temple to Richard Grenville of Wotton in 1710 united two of the most powerful Buckinghamshire families. Their increased status was reflected in an ever larger house at Stowe and in the control of elections so that members of the family or their nominees invariably occupied one or both of the Buckingham seats in Parliament, starting with Sir Peter Temple in 1639.

In 1604, Sir Thomas Temple bought the freehold of the manor of Buckingham which had been reserved in the 1573 lease of the manor to the Corporation by Bernard Brocas. The Temples thereafter regarded themselves as lords of the manor of Buckingham and continued to buy property in the town as it came on the market. About 1803, the Marquis of Buckingham was able to buy from Lord Sackville the land between the Brackley Road and Chackmore where he built Castle Fields Farm. In 1824 his son, now Duke of Buckingham, bought the manorial rights to the Prebend End and Gawcott from the Coke family, successors to the Dentons of Hillesden. The Temples, and the Grenvilles after them, sought to buy property in other Buckinghamshire towns like Aylesbury, and in other parts of the country, in order that their group in Parliament had plenty of rotten boroughs to return its members.

The bizarre electoral arrangements of Buckingham, where the franchise was limited to the bailiff and 12 members of the Corporation, were exposed in a report on the Corporation of Buckingham in 1833. It listed the following members of the Corporation in 1830 and their relationship to the Duke of Buckingham:

George Nelson (bailiff)	Formerly clerk to Mr Box, the banker to the late Marquis
John King	Attorney to the Duke
John Fellowes sen.	A tenant of the Duke
George Parrott	Steward of the Duke
John Fellowes jun.	Clerk to Mr Parrott, the Duke's steward
Charles Thomas Grove	Tenant of the Duke and paymaster of the Bucks Militia
James Masters	Quartermaster of the Bucks Militia
John Loveridge	Tenant of the Duke, and formerly adjutant of the Bucks Militia
Samuel Thomas	Late landlord of the *Cobham Arms Inn*, and tenant of the Duke
Thomas Swain	Landlord of the *Cobham Arms Inn*, and tenant of the Duke
James Harrison	Tenant of the Duke
George King	Tenant of the Duke and his draper
Christopher Dalton Bennett	The Duke's Grocer

The report stated that the Corporation 'served as an instrument for enabling the patron of the borough to return two Members to Parliament'. The Corporation even met in town halls paid for by the rival political families. Sir Ralph Verney is said to have paid for the Town Hall built in front of the *White Hart Inn* in 1685. The present Town Hall on the corner of the Market Square and Castle Street was built at the expense of George Grenville, Earl Temple, in 1783.

After the 1832 Reform Act, the boundaries of the Borough were extended to include the neighbouring parishes of Maids Moreton, Thornborough, Padbury, Hillesden, Preston Bissett, Tingewick and Radclive. This was designed to increase the number of electors and make bribing them too expensive. The Duke of Buckingham already had land holdings in most of these parishes, however, and his tenants still accounted for over a quarter of the electorate. He also had considerable influence over tradesmen in the town who depended on his custom. The financial collapse of the Duke and the 1848 sale of the contents of Stowe marked the end of the Duke's political control of Buckingham, but his son remained M.P. for the town until 1857. The second Reform Act reduced the number of members for Buckingham from two to one and from 1885 Buckingham was merged with the northern or Buckingham division of the county.

Buckingham in the 20th Century

The electoral reforms of the 19th century left Buckingham as a small municipal borough represented by a mayor, six aldermen and 12 councillors meeting at a Town Hall designed to hold the county assizes. The affairs of the surrounding villages were from 1895 in the hands of a Rural District Council which met in the board room of the Workhouse. The population of the town, which had increased rapidly to 4,054 in 1841, had fallen back to 3,152 by 1901. The tanneries and the brewery had closed down, but the boot factory remained and the agricultural machinery works had become a condensed milk factory.

There was little building work in Buckingham until Lloyd George's post-First World War government decreed that 'homes fit for heroes' should be built. Local councils were to assess housing need and seek to grants from central government to meet any shortfall. Council houses were built in Addington Road, east of the Workhouse, at Gawcott and at Bourton, where a street built in 1925-6 was named Bourtonville, recalling the Bournville garden suburb around the Cadbury chocolate factory in Birmingham. Some of the houses still have plaques recording the date of the housing scheme and the name of the mayor at the time.

By 1931, the population was still only 3,164. The Second World War brought about real change as both people and industry were evacuated from London. E. & F. Richardson, paint manufacturers from Mitcham in Surrey, took over the old Castle Mill in 1939. Leslie Hartridge Ltd., makers of diesel testing equipment at Enfield, moved to Buckingham in 1940. Other firms followed, their workers giving a much needed boost to trade in the town and to the local housing market. In 1959, Wipac, makers of car accessories, built a new factory on the London Road.

The policy of council house building continued after the Second World War. A new road was built connecting West Street with the Moreton Road and, by 1960, 250 more houses had been constructed.

Buckingham's development was still modest compared with Aylesbury and Bletchley whose agreements to take London overspill population meant that the Greater London

Council was building their roads and houses for them. Milton Keynes Development Corporation was formed in 1967 to create a new city of 250,000 and Buckingham wanted a share of this investment. In 1966, Buckingham Borough Council agreed an informal plan with the County Council for the future increase of population to 15,000. The Page Hill estate was started in 1970 under this plan. It was hoped that the Labour government's Land Commission might be persuaded to assemble further land for the plan, but the new Conservative government of 1970 abolished the Commission.

The solution was the Buckingham Development Company, promoted by Buckingham Borough Council and the County Council. Set up in 1971, it was to buy land by agreement with the owners, put in roads and sewers, and to sell land in parcels to developers according to an agreed expansion plan. The original landowners were to receive a proportion of the profits when the cost of servicing the land had been met, but about 25 per cent of the profit was to be spent on laying out public open space and building community facilities. The Badgers and Stratford Fields estates, with 440 houses, were built under this scheme and the first part of a new ring road was opened in 1979.

It was perhaps the combination of old-world charm and obvious potential which persuaded the promoters of the independent university to choose Buckingham as their site. The University of Buckingham was opened by Margaret Thatcher in 1976. Older buildings like the Roman Catholic College on the London Road and the former tannery on Hunter Street were converted and new halls of residence were built. The former agricultural machinery works on Chandos Road has been restored and is soon to become the university library. The old Town Mill has become the university refectory and the Congregational chapel in Church Street has become a lecture theatre. Negotiations are proceeding for the purchase of other buildings for teaching and administrative use.

The reorganisation of local government in 1974 put a brake on Buckingham's political aspirations if not on its expansion plan. The town was to become part of Aylesbury Vale District, its interests upheld by only three councillors on a council of 58 made up largely of representatives of rural communities. Buckingham's worst fears appeared to be confirmed when the new authority proposed to demolish the Town Hall in 1975 and sold off the council offices at Castle House in 1978. The reformed Town Council, with very limited powers, successfully opposed the destruction of the 18th-century Town Hall, but the building was sold and alternative facilities provided in a new community centre south of the High Street. Retailers were powerless to oppose the opening of a Tesco superstore on part of the Wipac site in 1993, which has drained income from the town centre.

Buckingham's population in 1991 was under 10,000. Aylesbury, its old rival for the status of county town, had now reached a population of over 51,000 and housing estates had spilled out beyond its boundary into the surrounding villages. Successive efforts of Edward the Confessor, Brown Willis, Lord Cobham and the Buckingham Development Company have failed to establish Buckingham as the premier town in the county. The current review of local government, likely to be implemented in 1997, is unlikely to change Buckingham's position as a small market town administered from distant Aylesbury. Its future must lie in developing its own institutions, like its independent university, and in preserving an identity separate from that of its larger neighbours.

1 The Anglo-Saxon Chronicle records the fortification of Buckingham against the Danes in 914. The promontory of high land surrounded on three sides by the river Ouse provided a natural defensive site. As with most fortifications, Buckingham's castle was redundant as soon as the battle moved on but its site, now occupied by the parish church, affords impressive views of the town and surrounding countryside.

2 Nothing remains of the medieval castle at Buckingham but some of the houses around the base of Castle Hill, such as these cottages on Nelson Street have unusually large blocks of stone in their foundations.

Bochingeha pro una hida se defd̄ T.R.E. & modo similr̄ facit. t̃ra ē viii. caruca̅. In dn̄io sun̄. ii. 7 uilli hn̄t. iii. car̄ 7 dim̄. 7 adhuc fr̄. 7 dim̄ poss̄ fieri. ibi sunt xx vi burgenses. 7 xu bord. 7 ii. serui. ibi. i. molin de xxiii. sol. p̃ti. viii. car̄. pasta ad pecuñ uille. In totis ualent̄ T.R.E. reddeb̄. xx. lib̄ ad numeru̅ Modo redd̄ xvi. lib̄ de albo argento.

De eadem hui̅ burgi ten̄ R. emiri ep̃s 7 t̃ra iiii. car̄ quae ad eā ptin̄. ibi sunt. iiii. car̄. 7 ii. uilli 7 u bord. 7 x. coti 7 i. molin. x. solid. p̃ti ii. car̄. Nem ad sepes. Valet 7 ualuit vii. lib̄. T.R.E. vii. lib̄. hanc eadem tenuit Wluui ep̃s de rege. E.

In hoc burgo ep̃s constantiensis hr̄. iii. burg̃ses. quos tenuit Wluuard fil̄ Esseue. hi reddu̅t vi. sol̄ vi. den̄. p annu̅. 7 regi redd̄ xii. den̄. Hugo comes hr̄. i. burgsem. q̃ fuit h̃o Burcardi. hic redd̄ xx vi. den̄. p annu̅. 7 regi v. denar̄. Robt̄ de Olgi hr̄. i. burg̃ qui fuit h̃o Azor. f. Totī. hic redd̄ xxvi. den̄. 7 regi v. denar̄. Roger̄ de Juri hr̄. iiii. burg̃ qui fuer̄ h̃oes Azar. hi redd̄ vii. sol̄ 7 vi. den̄. 7 regi xii. denar̄. Hugo de bolebec hr̄. iiii. burg̃ qui fuer̄ h̃oes Alriti. hi redd̄ xx viii. den̄. 7 regi xii. denar̄. Manno brito hr̄. iiii. burg̃ qui fuer̄ h̃o Esseue femine Sy̅ret. hi redd̄ xx xx den̄. regi nil deb. Walcouf musard hr̄. i. burg̃. qui fuit h̃o Azor. hic redd̄ xvi. den̄. 7 regi ii. denar̄. Ernulf de hesding hr̄. i. burg̃ qui fuit Wilaf. hic redd̄ p annu̅. ii. sol̄ 7 regi iiii. den̄. Wills de castellon de feudo ep̃i baiocensis hr̄. ii. burg̃. qui fuer̄ h̃oes Leuuini comit̄. hi redd̄ xvi. den̄. 7 regi in nichil. sed T.R.E. redd̄. iii. den̄. De feudo Alberti com̄. i. burg̃ redd̄ regi ii. den̄. Leuuin de Nuueha hr̄. v. burg̃. 7 T.R.E. habuit. hi redd̄ ii. iiii. sol̄ p annu̅. 7 regi xii. den̄.

3 Buckingham as the county town has pride of place in the Buckinghamshire Domesday. In 1086 it was a borough belonging to the king who had 26 burgesses there. Another 27 burgesses are mentioned as tenants of 11 different landlords, each of whom owned manors around Buckingham, suggesting ancient obligations to defend the town.

4 Buckingham's burgesses had the right to elect two Members of Parliament and their votes were often influenced by the generosity of politicians who had nearby estates. The Verneys of Claydon provided a town hall in 1685 but this was pulled down in 1783 and the present building erected on a site belonging to the Temple-Grenville family of Stowe.

5 The Town Hall had open arches on the ground floor and a large room above fitted out for holding the summer assizes. Its unbalanced appearance stems from the extension to the south wall and the rebuilding of the north wall in order to widen Castle Street.

6 The Temples also provided Buckingham's gaol as part of a campaign to regain the status of county town which had been lost to Aylesbury. The gaol was built in 1748 to coincide with the resumption of the Summer Assizes at Buckingham.

7 The semi-circular wing at the front of the gaol was added in 1839 to provide accommodation for the superintendent. Despite this further expenditure, Buckingham Gaol held few prisoners and an Act of Parliament returning the Summer Assizes to Aylesbury was passed in 1849.

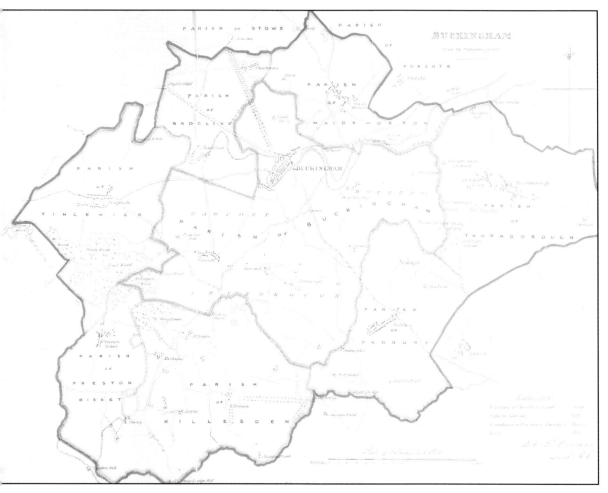

8 Prior to the 1832 Reform Act, Buckingham's bailiff and 12 burgesses had elected two Members of Parliament. Of these, 11 were tradesmen serving, or renting property from, the Duke of Buckingham. This map of 1831 shows how the borough boundary was extended to include the neighbouring parishes, whose electorate would be harder to manipulate.

9 The 1831 map shows Bourton as a village within the parish of Buckingham. It is separately mentioned in Domesday as having two ploughs at work. Its great manor house belonging to the Catholic Minshull family was destroyed during the Civil War, but Manor Farm, shown here, remains near the site. As with all farms of the hamlet, its land would originally have been scattered in strips in the open fields.

10 Bourton's manorial corn mill on the river Ouse also survives. The farmers of the hamlet would be obliged to grind their corn here.

11 White House Farm is one of several new farms created when the Minshulls enclosed Bourton in the 17th century. It is approached by a long private driveway which crosses ridge and furrow surviving from the old common fields.

12 White House Farm was probably built soon after the enclosures, but the present house is the result of rebuilding in the early 19th century.

13 Lenborough is also part of the parish of Buckingham and is assessed at Domesday for four ploughs. Lenborough lost most of its population after enclosure but its manor farm remains at what must have been the centre of the village.

14 Buckingham's castle may have served as a manor house as well as a stronghold. It is not to be equated with Castle House, on West Street, originally the home of the Bartons. It was John Barton, a Recorder of the City of London, who in his will of 1431 provided for the almshouses in Church Street. Castle House probably took its name from the nearby Castle Farm and Castle Mill.

15 The land attached to Castle House was scattered in strips in the open fields which lay to the north of the town, bordering Chackmore and Maids Moreton. Stowe Avenue was built after the enclosure of Chackmore in 1773 and crosses these former common fields. The avenue replaced a winding road to Chackmore which lay further to the east.

16 This farmhouse, now called the Corner House, stands at the junction of West Street and School Lane. It may well be the site of the Castle Farm, the home farm of the king and his successors as lords of Buckingham. It too had its land dispersed around the open fields of the town.

17 Castle Mill, Buckingham's manorial corn mill, stood by the Castle bridge which carries the Tingewick Road into the town. The mill was badly damaged by fire in November 1964 and only the proprietor's house now remains.

18 The area around the castle was, until recent times, known as Bourton Hold, Bourton meaning farm by the fort. This ancient farmhouse in Church Street is on the southern boundary of Bourton Hold.

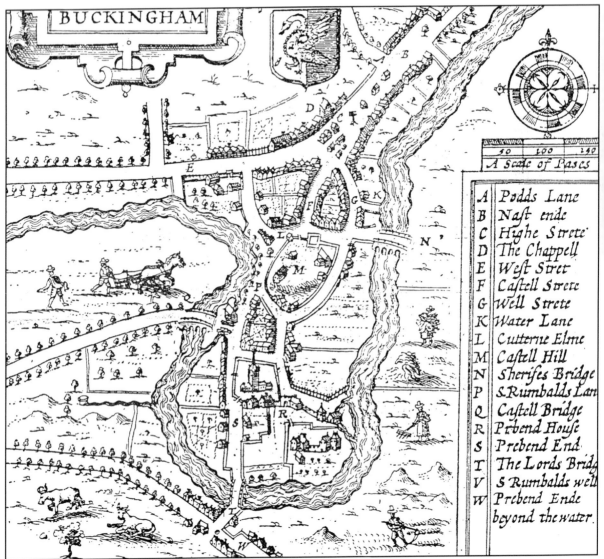

19 Speed's 1610 Map of the County of Buckingham includes this detail of the town of Buckingham. He represents the agricultural aspect of the town as well as marking the castle site and the market place. Of special note is the Prebendal House, the complex of buildings to the south east of the church. This was the centre of another Buckingham estate which from the time of Domesday until the Reformation had belonged to the Bishop of Lincoln, who gave the income from it to a Prebendary at Lincoln Cathedral.

20 Gawcott too belonged to the Bishop of Lincoln at Domesday and formed a manor with the 'Prebend End' of Buckingham. After the Reformation this manor was purchased by the Denton family of Hillesden. The Dentons supported the king during the Civil War and their great house at Hillesden was destroyed by the Parliamentary army. It is likely that the Prebendal House in Buckingham suffered the same fate.

21 The Dentons and their descendants continued to own the manor of the Prebend End with Gawcott until 1824 when it was purchased by the Duke of Buckingham. The Duke already owned this house in Church Street and, because he began to hold the manorial courts here, it became known as the Manor House.

22 A much photographed feature of the Manor House is the twisted chimney, partly of 16th-century construction with a later, possibly 18th-century shaft built against it.

23 The boundary between the town of Buckingham and the Prebend End is a straight line running along the north side of the Vicarage Garden, crossing Church Street here in front of the vicarage and continuing to the Castle bridge.

Church Street, Buckingham.

4 The vicarage may date from 1445 when the first vicar was appointed to take care of the spiritual needs of Buckingham on behalf of the Prebendary. The timber-framed house was rebuilt in the 17th century and extensively repaired in 1808.

25 The Prebend End of Buckingham had its own water mill to grind the corn of the lord of the manor's own tenants. The mill became known as 'Town Mill' and is now part of the University of Buckingham.

26 The Prebend End of Buckingham included the houses south of the bridge taking Hunter Street over the river Ouse. This area was called Church End with three public houses, a mission room and a Primitive Methodist chapel. The cottages on the right have been demolished but a surviving house on the corner has recently been found to be of cruck-framed construction.

27 This pasture land to the south of the river Ouse was part of the Great Port Field, one of the three common arable fields of the Prebend End of Buckingham. The ridges thrown up as a result of each farmer ploughing his separate strip of land can still be seen nearly 200 years after the three-field system was abandoned.

These meadows between Chandos Road and the river Ouse were once part of the Little Port Field, one of the three common arable fields of the Prebend End of Buckingham.

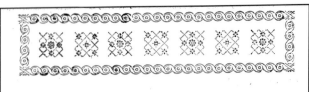

AN
A C T
FOR

Dividing and Inclofing the Open and Common Fields, Meadows, Paftures, and Wafte Grounds, within the Manor and Parifh of *Maidsmorton*, and the Hamlets of *Gawcott* and *Prebend-End*, in the Parifh of *Buckingham*, in the County of *Bucks*.

Ⓦ ☙☙☙☙☙ there are within the Manor and Parifh of *Maidsmorton*, and the Hamlets of *Gawcott* and *Prebend-End*, in the Parifh of *Buckingham*, in the County of *Bucks*, feveral Open and Common Fields, Meadows, Paftures, and Wafte Grounds:

And whereas the Moft Honourable *George Grenville Nugent Temple*, Marquis of *Buckingham*, Knight of the Moft Noble Order of the Garter, is Lord of the Honour of *Gloucefter* in *Maidsmorton*, and claims to be Lord of the Manor there, and is alfo Lord of the Manor of the Parifh of *Buckingham*, and feifed or poffeffed of the Impropriate or Rectorial Tythes arifing from the greater Part of the Lands lying within the faid Hamlets of *Gawcott* and *Prebend-End*, in the faid Parifh of *Buckingham*; and *John Bartlett* and others are feifed or poffeffed of the Refidue of fuch Tythes:

And whereas the Dean and Chapter of *Chrift Church*, in the Univerfity of *Oxford*, and *Samuel Churchill*, Efquire, their Leffee, are

A   feifed

29   The Prebend End with Gawcott was enclosed follow[ing] an Act of Parliament of 1801, which also provided for [the] enclosure of Maids Moreton. The Marquis of Buckingh[am] was the prime mover in this as part lord of the manor [of] Maids Moreton and owner of the right to collect tithes [(a] tenth of all farmers' crops formerly paid to the church) [in] the Prebend End and Gawcott.

30   The enclosure commissioners' award allotted new blocks of land to the farmers of the Prebend End and Gawcott who had previously had their land scattered in the open fields. The map which accompanies the award has this detail of the Prebend End.

1 One of the leading farmers in Gawcott at the time of the enclosure was William Eagles whose farmhouse, with two dormer windows, is on the left of this picture. At the enclosure he was able to exchange his scattered strips for a large block of land behind his house.

2 As a hamlet of Buckingham, Gawcott did not have its own church until 1806 when John West, a local lace dealer, paid for the erection of a chapel. This was replaced in 1828 by the present church.

33 The new church at Gawcott was in the classical style. The clear glass of the large windows give plenty of light to the nave.

34 This plaque in Gawcott church records the contribution to parish life of the Rev. Thomas Scott, the curate of Gawcott in 1828. His son, George Gilbert Scott, was to become the leading church architect of the Victorian period.

In a Vault beneath are interred the remains
of the Revd THOMAS SCOTT. M.A.
(Son of the late Rev.^d THO.^s SCOTT, Rector of Aston Sandford,)
and first Incumbent of this Chapelry.

For more than twenty seven years he discharged the functions
of this Office, and by the assistance of friends, tho' not without
considerable personal expence, he provided a commodious parsonage
and erected this Edifice, on the site of the former Chapel
which had fallen to decay.

Possessed of Enlarged understanding, unwearied diligence,
and very remarkable frankness of manners and benevolence of heart,
he dedicated all his powers to the service of his Saviour,
and the welfare of the flock committed to his charge.

By the kindness of the Lord Bishop of Lincoln he was presented
in 1833 to the Rectory of Wappenham, in Northamptonshire,
where he died Feby 24.th 1835, in the 55.th year of his age.

This Tablet is erected by a few of his most intimate friends,
in token of grateful remembrance and affectionate regret.

5 This 1840s print of the Market Hill emphasises Buckingham's position as an assize town (the newly extended gaol is prominent on the right) and features four members of the Royal Bucks Yeomanry, financed and controlled by the Duke of Buckingham.

36 The building plots to the south-east of Buckingham's Market Square all slope down to the river Ouse and seem to be the product of medieval town planning.

37 (*above left*) Several owners used the land behind their houses fronting the market area to build cottages for rent. These cottages were known as Meadow Row.

38 (*left*) Buckingham's Market Square would originally have been more open but as certain stalls became permanent there was considerable encroachment of houses and shops into the market place. The largest group of such buildings is this terrace of shops on the north-west of the Market Square.

39 (*above right*) Traders in the same goods tended to congregate in particular areas of the market place. Behind the shops on the north of the Market Square stood a wool hall. This was replaced in 1814 by a covered area for butchers and the north-west of Market Hill was known as Butchers' Row.

40 (*above*) Besides the Saturday market there were several fairs during the year, notably a wool fair in June, a sheep fair in September and a fatstock fair in December. Here the animals are penned in with temporary hurdles during the sheep fair in 1906. There was also a 'runaway fair' in the Autumn for hiring farm servants.

41 (*right*) The hairdresser's shop and saddlery in the centre of this view comprise another part of the market place called the Bull Ring.

42 (*above*) A closer view of Herring's saddlery in the Bull Ring.

43 There is a distinct absence of Victorian buildings in Buckingham, particularly in Market Square. This view shows almost exclusively late 18th- or early 19th-century shop fronts.

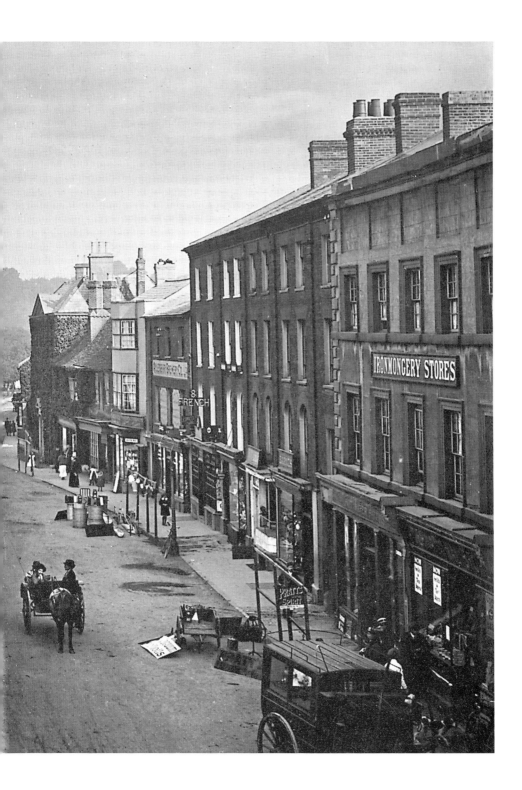

44 Some of the best houses fronting th Market Hilll were lost in the 1960s. Th prosperous 18th-century façade wit Venetian windows and classical pedimen was replaced by a branch of Woolworth

45 A new branch of Woolworths wa built on the site of 11-12 Market Hill. opened in 1964. Further shops are unde construction in the background.

46 Most of these buildings on Market Hill were demolished to build branches of Boots the Chemist and the Midland Bank.

47 These ancient houses of the lower side of Market Hill had fine 16th-century wall paintings. They were demolished for the building of the National Westminster Bank.

48 (*above*) The lower part of the market area was known as the North East End, Nast End or Cow Fair. *Pigot's Directory* of 1830 enthused that the Monday market, held in the Cow Fair, was 'one of the largest in the kingdom for calves'.

49 (*above*) There were several public houses in the Cow Fair. The inn sign is that of the *Horse and Groom* and beyond the cart entrance are the bay windows of the *Old Angel*.

50 (*left*) The decline of the market in the 19th century is evidenced by the planting of trees in the Cow Fair in 1872.

51 The original *Kings Head* inn was on the north side of the Cow Fair. It was demolished to widen the road to Maids Moreton and the licence was transferred to the present pub.

52 The house adjoining the old *Kings Head* has been restored and converted into a restaurant. The close studded timbering of the jettied upper floor has been revealed by the removal of the plaster.

The Twenty Policies following Deli:
vered to Mr. Caleb Gedney Riding Officer
at his going to Buckingham 17th March 1724

March 25th 1725

35081   William Dradge of Buckingham Tanner, for his
Dwelling house and Brewhouse, Barns & other Outhouses
adjoyning to the Same and for his Goods and Merchan:
dize inclosed in the Same and for two Houses near
the Same all Situate in the Town aforesaid as herein
after particularly express'd only.

Dwelling house & Brewhouse only 200. Goods in Do. 60   260

One Bark Barn only 20. Two Barns only 20   40

One Tan Barn 20 Goods in the Bach barn only 100   120

Goods in the Two Barns 20. Do. in the Tan Barn 20   40

One House in the Possession of Samuel Evans   20

And one House in the Possession of Jo: Goodall   20

3/   500

March 25

35082   John Harrison of the Town of Buckingham, Fellmonger:
for his now Dwelling house, Warehouse & Chambers over it
Wool house & Stable, Workhouse & other Outhouses all adjoyn:
Situate in the Town aforesaid and for his Goods and Merchan:
dize enclosed in the same & for two Houses Situate in the
Said Town with the Barns belonging to the Same as herein
after particularly express'd only and not elsewhere.

For the Dwelling house only 250. Goods in Do. 50.   300

One Warehouse & Chamber over it adj: 30. Goods in Do. 60.   90

A Woolhouse & Stable 60. Goods in Do. 60.   120

A Workht in the Same Yd by the river Side 30. Goods in Do. 10.   40

Three Bays of Building 20. One house now in Possession of — Tho: Allen 30. One Woolhouse adjoyning 20.   70

One house now in Possession of Will. Brighton & Tho: Baldin   120

Two Barns belonging to the Same   60

5/   800

53 A fire on 15 March 1724-25 consumed 138 of Buckingham's 387 houses. It is said to have begun at the *Unicorn Inn* in the Market Square and to have progressed along Castle Street and Well Street. Two days later an officer of the Sun Insurance sold 20 policies to those whose property was spared.

54 To accommodate some o
those made homeless by th
1724 fire, the Red Building
were put up in the Cow Fai
the money provided by th
Temple family of Stowe. T
houses remained until 1866.

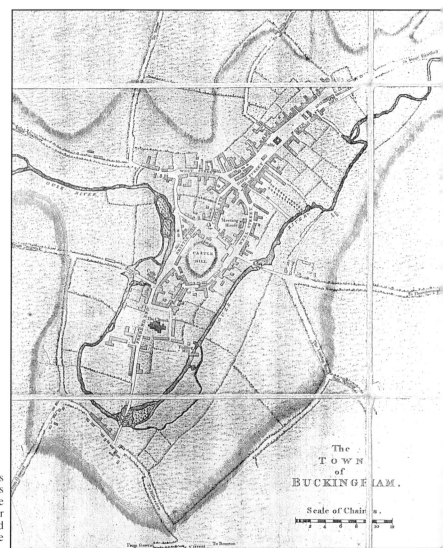

The
TOWN
of
BUCKINGHAM.

Scale of Chain[ ]s.

55 Jeffery's map of 1770 shows
the Red Buildings as two blocks
in the 'North East End' of the
town. The map is noteworthy for
showing the two water mills and
the vacant castle site prior to the
building of the new church.

6 As Castle Street was largely destroyed in the fire of 1725, all the buildings here date from the 18th century and include several fine brick houses.

57 Trolley Hall was rebuilt after the fire by Charle[s] Blunt, an ironmonger. It was later occupied by Newma[n] Williat, a lace buyer, and then by Thomas Bartlett, partner in the Buckingham Bank.

58 Some of the façades have been altered t[o] accommodate Victorian and more modern shop front[s]. The draper Albert Vyles was responsible for thi[s] transformation.

9 As a market town lacking any raw material like coal or iron ore, Buckingham's industries were bound to be related to agriculture. The Castle Mill, one of three water corn mills in the town, was rebuilt in 1897 and operated until the 1930s. It was destroyed by fire in 1964.

60 Town Mill had two large water wheels drivi six pairs of stones. The mill is now part of Buckingha University, an institution that has provided new us for several old buildings in the vicinity.

61 Town Mill has the datestone WK 1782. T initials are those of William King whose family we millers, bakers and dyers. On Jeffery's map the m is marked as a fulling mill, suggesting that Willia King had fulling stocks for finishing locally wov cloth, as well as millstones for grinding corn.

62 The weir serving Town Mill can be seen in the river below the bridge carrying Hunter Street over the Ouse. The bridge was rebuilt when the construction of the railway embankment led to the Ouse being diverted in 1846.

63 Bourton Mill was powered by a single water wheel turning four pairs of stones. It was last operated in the 1920s and is now used as a health club.

64 Another industry common to market towns was that of malting. Locally grown barley was converted into malt for sale to local publicans who brewed their own beer, or in the 19th century, to common or wholesale brewers who often had tied pubs over a wide area. These maltings on the Lenborough Road were built about 1865 and belonged to the Gough family.

65 The oldest brewery in the town was that of the Stutchbury family, situated here in the North End of Buckingham. The brewery occupied a site roughly where the Masonic Hall was built in 1890.

The Swan Brewery dates at last from the 1840s. By the 1860s was run by John Terry, whose family ran the Walton Brewery in Aylesbury. Terry and his successor, Frank Higgens, had several tied pubs the vicinity of Buckingham.

67 The Swan Brewery was taken over in 1896 by the Aylesbury Brewery Co. and in 1904 was converted to an electric light works.

68 The large house on West Street was the home of Richard Elkington, a wine and spirit merchant and hop dealer. Some of his outbuildings and garden were across the road to the north of Market Hill. The business was later run by the Bennett family who were also estate agents in the town.

69 Any town with a cattle market can be expected to have tanneries. In the 18th century the Buckingham tanners were grouped in the Prebend End of the town and the tanyards occupied the land between Hunter Street and the river. Norton House is so named after one of the leading tanning families.

70 Prebend House, on Hunter Street, was built by the Bartletts, the most opulent of the tanning families, and is not to be confused with the Prebendal House which once stood south of the old churchyard. John Bartlett, who died in 1826 and is buried in the family vault across the road in the churchyard, was a partner with Philip Box in Buckingham's first bank.

71 One of the biggest buildings associated with the tannery was this wooden structure to the south west of Prebend House. It was demolished in 1974.

72 Yeomanry House, so named because it later became the headquarters of the Royal Bucks Yeomanry, was also owned by the Bartletts. When the family sold their tanyards, Frederick Edward Bartlett continued in business here as a woolstapler, employing over 20 men and boys. This trade also declined as it became the practice to send fleeces direct to the Yorkshire woollen towns rather than to sort the wool locally.

73 With the opening of the railway to Buckingham in 1850, the Castle Iron Works was built to make agricultural machinery. It became well known for its steam-powered road vehicles but the firm failed in 1865. The building later became a corn mill and then a condensed milk factory. It is soon to be the library of Buckingham University.

4 The ironmonger's premises on the right of this photograph were formerly occupied by Henry Holland, a successful shoemaker. Through the entry on the left of his premises is a four-storey shoe factory, recently converted into luxury flats.

75 The shoe factory is built of yellow brick of a type which only appeared in Buckingham after the construction of the railway in 1850.

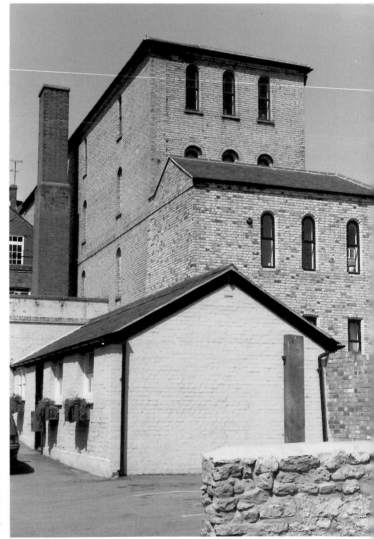

76 The shoe factory features in Flora Thompson's *Lark Rise to Candleford*. Flora Thompson (née Timms) was born in 1876 at Juniper Hill, a hamlet of Cottisford, seven miles west of Buckingham. The shoemaker Rechab Holland was her uncle.

7 On the death of Philip Box in 1811, his partner John Bartlett formed his own bank which continued until 1853 when it amalgamated with banks in Aylesbury and Banbury to form the Bucks and Oxon Union Bank. The headquarters were here in Buckingham's Market Square. The bank was taken over by Lloyds in 1902.

8 Philip Box, who started the Buckingham Bank in 1786, probably operated from his own home. The Bank later had premises in the Town Hall. This one pound note was issued by Box's bank in 1815.

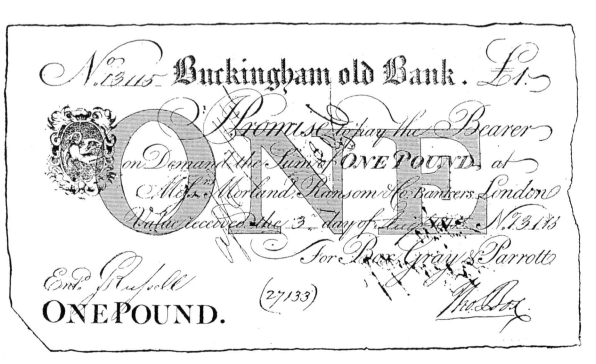

79   Inns are vital to market towns as they provide places for bargains to be struck on market day and food and rest for travellers and their horses. One of the leading inns in Buckingham was the *White Hart*; coaches used to enter the inn yard through an archway in the centre of the building but, with the end of the coaching era, this was converted in 1871 into a lobby.

The London coaches stopped at the *Cobham Arms* West Street. The inn belonged to the Temple-renville family of Stowe and was tenanted for over 0 years by the Baxter family. With the advent of ilways and the bankruptcy of the Duke of uckingham, it was closed and the building was sold 1856.

81 The narrow but tall entrance to the *Cobham Arms* is still in place and leads up a steep roadway to the site of the stables.

82 The façade of the former *George Inn*, now called the White House, is remarkably similar to that of the *Cobham Arms*. Both date from the mid-18th century when inns competed to win the mushrooming coaching trade. With the opening of the London to Birmingham railway in 1838, the coaching trade died. Coaches plied to and from the nearest railway station at Wolverton until Buckingham got its own line in 1850.

83 The *Swan and Castle* in Castle Street advertised itself as a posting house, meaning that it kept post horses ready to change the teams on the long distance coaches. As early as 1738, a sale notice described it as 'the White Swan in Buckingham, an ancient well accustomed house, stables 100 horses'.

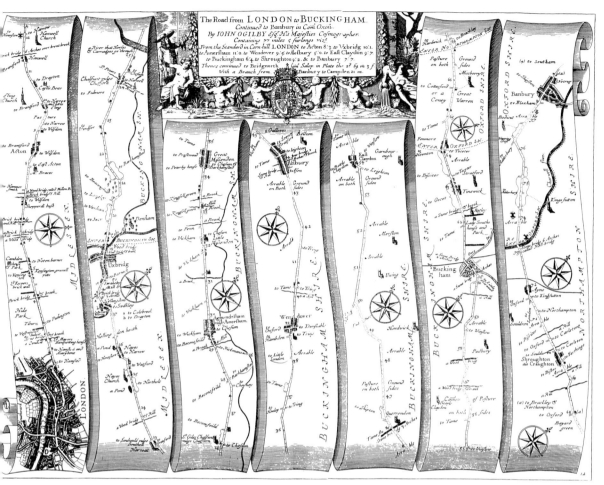

4 Whilst the coaching trade lasted, maps like this 1675 strip map by John Ogilby would be found at every inn. They showed the routes, the river crossing points and even the state of cultivation of the land on either side of the road. This map shows the line of the old coaching road from Aylesbury to Buckingham going through East Claydon rather than through Winslow, the route of the later turnpike road.

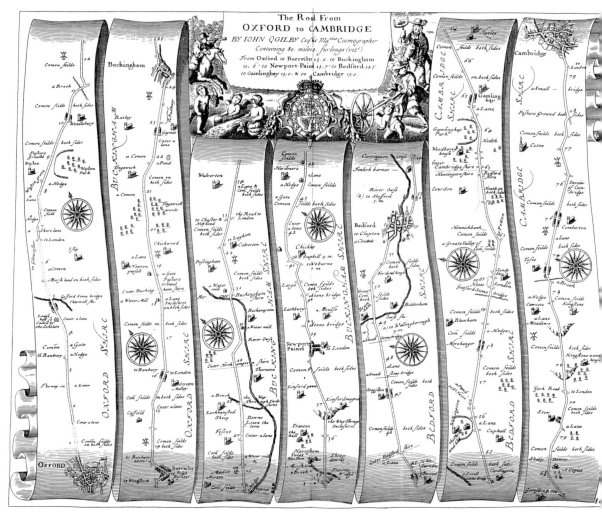

85   Another of Ogilby's maps shows the Oxford to Cambridge road passing through Buckingham and crossing the Ouse at Beachampton on its way to Newport Pagnell.

The Buckingham to Wendover road was one of the earliest turnpikes in the county. The Act of Parliament giving named trustees the right to levy tolls and to apply the proceeds to the repair of the road was passed in 1720. Amongst the promoters were gentry families like the Verneys of Claydon and the Lowndes of Winslow.

Anno Regni
GEORGII
REGIS
Magnæ Britanniæ, Franciæ, & Hiberniæ,
SEPTIMO.

At the Parliament Begun and Holden at *Westminster*, the Seventeenth Day of *March, Anno Dom.* 1714. In the First Year of the Reign of our Sovereign Lord *GEORGE*, by the Grace of God, of *Great Britain, France,* and *Ireland*, King, Defender of the Faith, *&c.*

And from thence Continued by several Prorogations to the Eighth Day of *December,* 1720. Being the Sixth Session of this present Parliament.

London, Printed by *John Baskett,* Printer to the King's most Excellent Majesty, And by the Assigns of *Thomas Newcomb,* and *Henry Hills,* deceas'd. 1721.

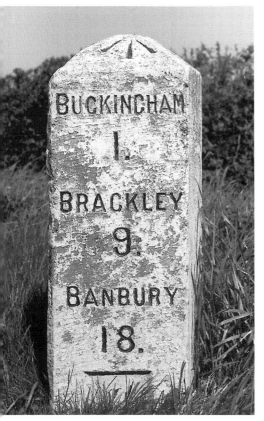

87 Milestones giving the distances to the principal towns were erected along the turnpike roads. This example is on the east side of the road opposite the entrance to Tesco's store.

88 The Buckingham to Wendover Turnpike entered the town via a six-arch stone bridge known as the Sheriff's bridge. The old route into the town was downgraded when a new bridge further down stream was built in 1805. The old road became a ford and a wooden foot bridge was provided, later to be replaced by a superior iron bridge. The *Woolpack Inn*, seen at the end of Ford Street in this view, suffered a loss of trade as a result of realigning the road.

9 The Well Street area of the town was always subject to flooding. Here the flood extends past the *Bull Inn* almost as far as the Board School.

90 The new bridge was called the 'London Road Bridge' or 'Long Bridge'. The Grenvilles of Stowe met the cost.

91 On the east side of the London Road bridge is the coat of arms of the Temple-Grenville family with the motto *Templa Quam Dilecta* and the date 1805.

92 A new road from the 1805 bridge to Well Street and so to the Market Square was appropriately named Bridge Street.

93 The *New Inn* and a terrace of houses were built on the approach to the bridge from the south.

94 The turnpike toll collector's house at Padbury was rebuilt in 1828 following the realignment of the road approaching Padbury bridge. It stood to the north west of the turn to Lenborough.

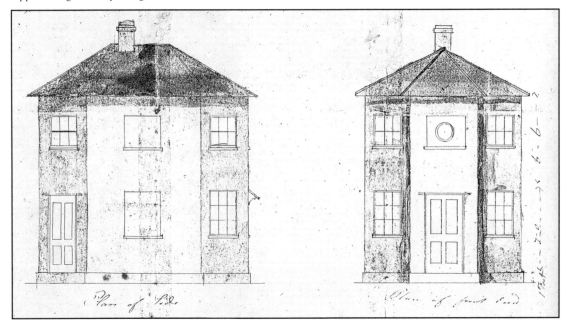

WENDOVER & BUCKINGHAM TURNPIKE
TRUST.

TO BUILDERS AND OTHERS.

GEORGE BENNETT

Is instructed by the Trustees, to SELL BY AUCTION

AT THE WHALE INN, IN BUCKINGHAM,

ON SATURDAY, NOVEMBER THE 2ND, 1878,

At Three for Four o'clock in the afternoon punctually.

THE WHOLE OF THE

Materials of the Toll House

With the GATES and FENCES, in the Hamlet of Lenborough, commonly called

PADBURY GATE.

PARTICULARS.

Lot

1. The 11ft. 6in. Turnpike Gate, with hanging and shutting post and fastening-open post and the railing and fencing, (as across the road leading to Lenboro').
2. The 12ft. Turnpike Gate, with hanging and shutting posts, lock and key, the latches and fastening-open posts. The Hand Gate and Post, fencing and turnstile, (as across the Turnpike road).
3. The Porch in front of the House with Doors, Lamp, 2 Toll Boards, 2 Flag Stones and Bricks.
4. The whole of the Brickwork forming the Erection of the Octagon Toll House, Barn and Closet.
5. The whole of the Slates, Spouting, and Lead, on roof of same.
6. The whole of the Roofing, Joists, and Floors of the same.
7. Five Doors and Frames, 6 Window Sashes, and 3 inside Shutters.
8. Small Range, Chimney Piece, Cupboard, and 2 Shelves.

☞ *May be Viewed at any time prior to the Sale, and Particulars obtained of Messrs. Tindal and Baynes, Clerks to the Trustees, Aylesbury, or of the Auctioneer, Buckingham.*

CONDITIONS.

1.—The Highest Bidder shall be the Purchaser, and if any dispute arise between two or more Bidders, the Lot in dispute shall be put up again and re-sold.

2.—No person to advance at each bidding a less sum than shall be named by the Auctioneer at the time of putting up each Lot.

3.—The Purchasers to pay the amount of their respective Lots to the Auctioneer immediately after the Sale.

4.—The Purchasers are to take down their respective Lots, and remove the materials thereof at their own expense and risk, but no Lot can be removed till after 12 o'clock on Monday the 4th of November next, and each Purchaser will be required to clear away his Lot or Lots within one week from that date, without damaging any other Lot.

5.—In digging out the Foundation, Paving, Posts, etc., the Purchaser will be required to properly fill in and level the ground.

6.—If any dispute or question should arise, between any Purchaser and the Trustees, respecting any purchase under these conditions, or the constructions of such conditions ; such dispute or question, shall be referred to the Auctioneer, whose decision thereon shall be conclusive on both parties.

LASTLY.—Should any Lot or Lots remain uncleared after the time limited in the fourth condition for removing the Lots, the purchase money of each Lot or Lots shall be forfeited to the Trustees, and the Lot or Lots in question re-sold either by Public or Private Sale, and the deficiency (if any) on such second Sale, together with all charges attending the same, shall be made good by the defaulter or defaulters at this Sale.

W. CARTER, PRINTER, "EXPRESS" OFFICE, BUCKINGHAM.

95 The toll collector's house was demolished when the last Buckingham to Wendover Turnpike Act expired in 1878. The materials of the building were auctioned, including the gate and the toll board.

96 The road via Tingewick to Banbury was improved following the 1744 Buckingham to Warmington Turnpike Act. Warmington is a village five miles north of Banbury where the road continued to the north under the control of another group of turnpike trustees.

97 The bridge carrying the Banbury road out of the town was called the Castle bridge and was adjacent to the Castle Mill. It was rebuilt about 1851.

This turnpike milestone, similar in pattern to those [on] the Buckingham to Wendover turnpike, is on the north [si]de of the road approaching Tingewick.

The Buckingham to Warmington Act specified that [th]ere should be a turnpike toll collector's house at [Dr]opshort, on the boundary of Buckingham and Radclive. [Th]is is shown on Jeffery's map of 1770.

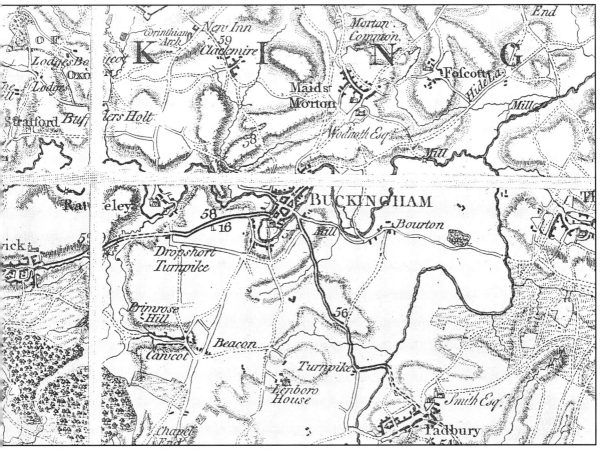

100 It was felt that the alternative route to Banbury via Brackley should also be maintained by turnpike trustees. An Act of Parliament was passed in 1791. The milestones on this road had cast-iron plaques giving the distances to the next town. None of the plaques remains in place today.

101 The next road to be improved was that to Newport Pagnell, turnpiked in 1815 as the Buckingham to Old Stratford Road. This print of 1801 shows the condition of the road prior to the Act creating the turnpike trust.

2 The milestones on the Newport Pagnell road are triangular in section
d are made of cast iron.

3 The road to Towcester was turnpiked as late as 1824. 'Our new road
much admired and reckoned not only of great utility but an ornament to
r vicinity', enthused the vicar of Stowe in a letter the following year.

04 This milestone on the turnpike road to Towcester still stands outside
he *Buckingham Arms* at Maids Moreton.

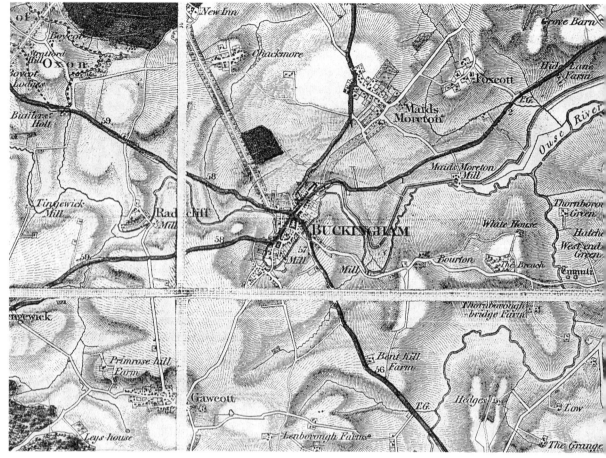

105 The turnpike roads radiating out of Buckingham are well illustrated on the Ordnance Survey map of 1834. Toll gates are shown at Padbury and Foscote.

6 A branch of the Grand Junction Canal from Old Stratford to Buckingham was opened in 1801. The line of the now disused canal can be seen just north of Thornborough Mill.

7 The canal passed close by Maids Moreton Mill where this lifting bridge survived into the 1930s.

108 The Old Wharf was some way out of Buckingham. Some canal-side cottages remain in 1994.

109 The wharfinger's house remains at the entrance to the New Wharf on the Stony Stratford Road. Perhaps because the Buckingham branch was built to accommodate narrow boats rather than barges, the canal was not heavily used. The railway brought in coal more efficiently than the canal, which was constantly silting up and was not in use by 1909.

110 The *Ship Inn* on the Cow Fair was rebuilt in 1802 and renamed the *Grand Junction Inn*.

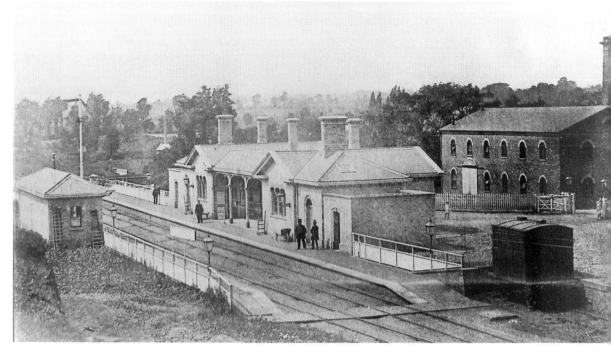

111 Buckingham might have developed more in the 19th century had it been on a main line railway. Instead it was served by a single line branch from Verney Junction, on the Bletchley to Oxford line, to a terminus at Banbury. The line was promoted by the Buckinghamshire Railway Company with the support of the London and North Western Railway. It was opened in 1850.

112 The Banbury branch was never a busy line. Here a train of only two coaches waits for departure for Bletchley in 1957.

13 Diesel railcars were introduced on the Banbury branch in 1956. Here a railcar is about to leave for Banbury whilst e steam 'push and pull' train is about to leave for Bletchley.

14 The economies made by the railcars were not sufficient to avoid the closure of the passenger service from Buckingham Banbury in 1960. Passenger services on the whole line closed in 1964 and the track was lifted in 1967.

115 Unlike many market towns, Buckingham did not enjoy a period of expansion on the opening of the railway. Chandos Road, linking the railway station with the London Road, is almost the only sign of Victorian prosperity.

116 Building plots along Chandos Road were developed slowly. These houses had been built by 1880.

117 House plots further along Chandos Road towards the railway station were not built on until the 1960s.

18 The grandest house on Chandos Road was Brookfield, a hunting box occupied at the turn of the century by Richard . Budgett, a noted sportsman and coaching enthusiast. Since 1963 it has formed part of the Royal Latin School.

The Town Arms

119 Buckingham church was large cruciform structure with spire 163ft. high. The woode spire fell in February 1698-9 badly damaging the tower. Th spire was not replaced but th tower was repaired in rudimentary manner.

120 In 1753 the tower o Buckingham church was raisec some 24ft. The join is obviou in this contemporary print. Th foundations of the original towe proved inadequate for the extr weight and the new tower fe in 1776.

1 It was decided in 1777 to rebuild the church on another site. The Verney family were persuaded to donate the site on the Castle Hill and the Grenvilles underwrote the cost of the new building. The new church, finished in 1781, had a large oblong nave with square tower and elegant stone spire. There was no chancel.

22 Inside the 18th-century church were galleries on three sides and a fine three-decker pulpit, putting the preacher in perfect position to be seen and heard.

123 19th-century tastes in church architecture reflected an interest in liturgy rather than preaching and it was thought essential to have a chancel on a church. When this was added to Buckingham church in 1865 the building was strengthened by the addition of substantial buttresses.

124 Inside the restored church galleries either side of the nave were removed and the whole character of the church transformed from 18th-century preaching house to Victorian Gothic.

125 The non-conformists in Buckingham met in houses licensed for the purpose until 1726 when this meeting house was built on Well Street. It became the 'Old Meeting House' from 1792 when part of the congregation left to form a new meeting in Church Street. From 1844 until 1876, the building housed Buckingham's British School.

126 The original meeting house in Church Street was built in 1793. The two groups of independents rejoined in 1850 and built this new church on the Church Street site in 1857. The building is now used by the University of Buckingham.

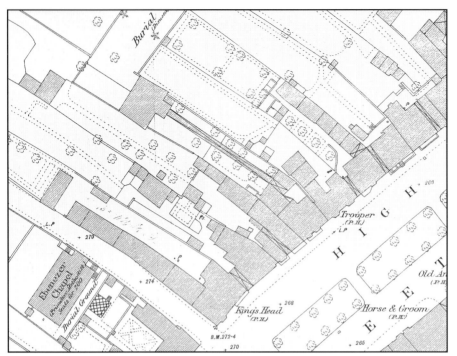

127 The Quaker Meeting H was built in 1786 in the garden house on the north side of the Fair belonging to the Coles fa who were bakers and watchm in Buckingham.

128 The Wesleyans built a chapel on Well Street in 1792. It was altered and enlarged several times before its replacement by the present church in 1968. Here the Wesleyans parade along Nelson Street, *c*.1910.

29 The Baptists were comparatively weak in Buckingham, only erecting this church in Moreton Road in 1842. Although one or two of the independents moved to the new church, the congregation dwindled until the building was given up in 1876. From 1876 to 1879, the chapel was used as a Board School, but since 1916 it has been used by the Salvation Army.

30 There is doubt about the antiquity of the Royal Latin School but it seems to have been funded from 1540 by a bequest of Isabel Denton of Hillesden. The school was housed in this former chantry chapel on the Market Hill.

131 During its life as a school, the chantry chapel wa[s] restored and altered but some of the masonry and the la[te] 12th-century Norman doorway have been preserved.

132 When the chapel was converted into a school after the Reformation, a schoolmaster's house was added to the north. This was rebuilt in 1696. Beyond the house is a three-storey addition built in the late 19th century to provide extra classrooms.

33 The 1902 Education Act allowed county education authorities to support old endowed grammar schools. In 1907 the Royal Latin School moved to new premises built by the county council on Chandos Road and for the first time admitted girls as well as boys. It moved again in 1963 to the present site at Brookfield.

134 These new buildings were erected when the Royal Latin school moved to the Brookfield site in 1963.

135 The National School was started in 1819, partly funded by the National Society for the Education of the Poor in the Principles of the Established Church. It was rebuilt in 1856 and a second storey was added in 1872. It was in use as a school until 1935.

136 The 1870 Education Act enabled towns to elect school boards which funded new schools with a special rate. Buckingham took up the scheme and the non-denominational Board School was built in Well Street in 1879.

7 The Well Street Board School was an elementary school until the building of the Secondary School in 1935. It remained in use as a primary school until 1991.

8 The County Council built a secondary school on the London Road in 1935. A 1970s plan to merge the school with the Royal Latin School to form a comprehensive was dropped and the two schools remain on adjacent sites.

139 Barton's Almshouses were funded by a bequest in the 1431 will of John Barton, who required his executor to house six poor men or women of Buckingham who would pray daily for his soul.

140 Under the 1834 Poor Law Amendment Act, 29 parishes were amalgamated into the Buckingham Poor Law Union. A new workhouse was built on the Stony Stratford Road, designed by George Gilbert Scott, the son of the curate at Gawcott, who later achieved fame as a church architect. The plan was almost exactly similar to this standard design used by the leading workhouse architect, Sampson Kempthorne, whose London office was next door to that of Scott.

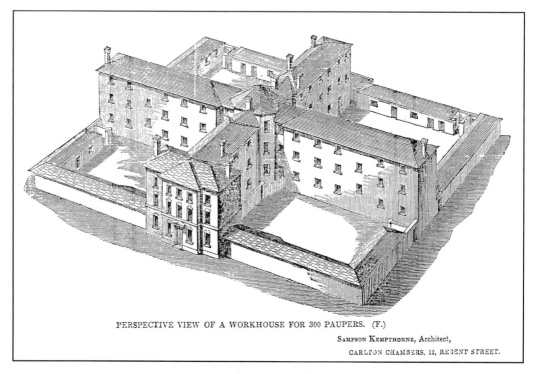

PERSPECTIVE VIEW OF A WORKHOUSE FOR 300 PAUPERS. (F.)

SAMPSON KEMPTHORNE, Architect,
CARLTON CHAMBERS, 12, REGENT STREET.

1 As part of the post First World War policy of 'homes fit for heroes', the national government required local authorities to assess housing need and to provide adequate housing. These council houses in Bourton Road were built by Buckingham Corporation in the 1920s.

2 Buckingham had a fine record in the construction of council housing. These houses, aptly named 'Bourtonville' after the Bournville garden suburb around the Cadbury factory in Birmingham, were built in 1925-26.

143 Further council houses were built by Buckingham Corporation here on Buckingham Road, Gawcott.

144 A plaque on the gable end of one of the council houses records that the Gawcott housing scheme was completed in the years 1926-27.

45   These houses in Western Avenue were built by Buckingham Borough Council after the Second World War. In all, the Borough Council built 625 homes.

46   This group of commercially built houses was named Portfield Way, recalling the name of one of the former open fields of the Prebend End of Buckingham on which it was built.

147 (*above*) The open-air swimming pool was built in 1955 below the London Road bridge. It is shown prior to reconstruction in 1977.

148 (*above*) Buckingham Football Club on their ground between Chandos Road and the river.

149 (*left*) Gawcott Cricket Club, photographed on the occasion of a match between the married and the single men of the village in 1911.

150 The Chandos Cinema was built on the corner of London Road and Chandos Road in 1934. It remained independent of any cinema chain until closure in 1987. It is now used as a car showroom and workshop.

151 A favourite Sunday afternoon walk was along Maids Moreton Avenue, planted along the driveway from the Stratford Road to The Manor, a large house belonging to the Andrewes family situated on the Maids Moreton boundary.

152 Stowe Avenue stretches for over a mile, connecting the palatial home of the Temple-Grenville family with the Borough of Buckingham which they sought to control.

153 Stowe house is built on the site of an earlier manor house which was in turn the focal point of the village of Stowe. Sir Richard Temple completed the enclosure of Stowe about 1649 and is probably responsible for the depopulation of the village.

154 The ridge and furrow created by the farmers of Stowe is clearly visible in this view of the park, featuring the Gothic Temple.

55 The tradition that Lord Cobham moved the residents of Stowe to Dadford (shown here) when Stowe gardens were laid out in the early 18th century, may in fact arise from the late 19th-century exodus from Lamport.

156 Behind the Palladian Bridge stood the manor house and village of Lamport. The estate was purchased in 1823 by the Duke of Buckingham and the manor house was demolished. As late as 1861 there were still 16 families living in the hamlet of Lamport but, by 1871, half of them had been moved to Dadford.

157 Such was the power of the Grenvilles that they funded their own regiment of Yeomanry Cavalry for which these Barracks on West Street were built in 1802.

ANNO DUODECIMO

VICTORIÆ REGINÆ.

****

C A P. VI.

An Act to repeal an Act of the Twenty-first Year of *George* the Second, for holding the Summer Assizes at *Buckingham ;* and to authorize the Appointment of a more convenient Place for holding the same. 　　　　[9th *March* 1849.]

WHEREAS by an Act passed in the Session of Parliament holden in the Twenty-first Year of the Reign of His late Majesty King *George* the Second, intituled *An Act for holding the Summer Assizes for the County of* Buckingham *at the County Town of* Buckingham, it was enacted, that from and after the First Day of *June* One thousand seven hundred and forty-eight all the Commissions of Assize and Nisi Prius, and all General Commissions of Oyer and Terminer, and all Commissions of General Gaol Delivery, which should thereafter be appointed to be held and executed for the said County next after the Term of *Holy Trinity*, should be held and executed in each Year at and in the said Town of *Buckingham*, and at no other Place within the said County of *Buckingham*, any Law, Statute, Usage, Matter, or Thing to the contrary notwithstanding : And whereas by an Act passed in the Session of

H

Parliament

---

158 Lord Cobham's move to build a new gaol and secure the return of the summer assizes to Buckingham by Act of Parliament in 1748 was successful for just one hundred years. In 1849, one year after the financial collapse of the Duke of Buckingham and the sale of the contents of Stowe, the 1748 Act was repealed and the assizes returned to Aylesbury, now the undisputed county town.

Bibliography

Baines, A. H. J. 'The development of the Borough of Buckingham, 914-1086'. *Records of Buckinghamshire* Vol. 27, 1985

Clarke, John *The book of Buckingham*, 1984

Davies, R. & Grant, M.D., *Forgotten railways: Chilterns and Cotswolds*, 1975

Davis, Richard W., *Political change and continuity 1760-1885, a Buckinghamshire study*, 1972.

Elliott, Douglas J., *Buckingham, the loyal and ancient borough*, 1975

Faulkner, Alan H., *The Grand Junction Canal*, 1972.

Harrison, J.T., *Leisure-hour notes on historical Buckingham*, 1909

Lipscomb, George, *History and antiquities of the County of Buckingham*

Pemberton, Joyce & Pemberton, John, *The University College at Buckingham*, 1979

Royal Commission on the Historical Monuments of England, *Non-conformist chapels and meeting houses: Buckinghamshire*, 1986

Victoria History of the County of Buckingham, 4 vols., 1905-27

Willis, Brown, T*he history and antiquities of the town, hundred and deanry of Buckingham*, 1755.

Index

Roman numerals refer to pages in the introduction and arabic numerals to individual illustrations.